Our Solar System

THE INNER PLANETS

Mary-Jane Wilkins
Consultant: Giles Sparrow, FRAS

WAYLAND
www.waylandbooks.co.uk

This edition first published in Great Britain
in 2016 by Wayland

© 2016 Brown Bear Books Ltd

Wayland
An imprint of Hachette Children's Group
Part of Hodder & Stoughton
Carmelite House
50 Victoria Embankment
London EC4Y 0DZ
An Hachette UK Company
www.hachette.co.uk
www.hachettechildrens.co.uk

ISBN 978 1 5263 0281 6

Brown Bear Books Ltd
First Floor, 9–17 St. Albans Place
London N1 0NX

Author: Mary-Jane Wilkins
Consultant: Giles Sparrow, Fellow of the Royal
Astronomical Society
Picture Researcher: Clare
Illustrations: Supriya Sahai
Designer: Melissa Roskell
Design Manager: Keith D
Editorial Director: Lindsey
Children's Publisher: Anne

Printed in Malaysia

Picture Credits
Front Cover: ©Shutterstock/Aphelleon /Quaoar/
Natalia Rashevska/Anton Balazh
Inside: 1, ©Shutterstock/Johan Swanepoel;
4, ©Shutterstock/Ixpert; 4-5, ©Shutterstock/Fluid
Workshop; 6, ©NASA/MSFC/Aaron Mingery; 6-7,
©Shutterstock/Maceij Sojka; 8, ©Shutterstock/
Vadim Sadocski; 8-9, ©Shutterstock/Mopic;
10, ©Shutterstock/Photo Platmicon; 10-11,
©Shutterstock/Mode List; 11, ©NASA; 12, ©NASA/
JHUAPL/Carnegie Institute; 12-13, ©NASA/
JHUAPL/Carnegie Institute; 14, ©Shutterstock/
Terrance Emerson; 14-15, ©Shutterstock/Tristan
3D; 16, ©NASA; 16-17, ©NASA/JPL; 18, ©NASA/
JPL/ISGS; 18-19, ©NASA; 19, ©NASA/JPL-Caltech/
University of Arizona; 20, ©NASA; 20-21, ©NASA/
JPL; 23, ©Shutterstock/Mopic.
T=Top, C=Centre, B=Bottom, L=Left, R=Right

Brown Bear Books has made every attempt
to contact the copyright holder. If you have
any information please contact:
licensing@brownbearbooks.co.uk

Websites
The website addresses (URLs) included in this
book were valid at the time of going to press.
                             ble that contents or addresses
                             wing the publication of this
                             bility for any such changes
                             by either the author or the

Contents

Where are the inner planets?

The inner planets are the four planets closest to the Sun in the solar system. They are Mercury, Venus, Earth and Mars.

Earth's atmosphere contains air. This makes it possible for us to live here.

All four planets have a layer of gases around them. This is called an atmosphere. Venus has a very thick one. On Mercury and Mars the atmosphere is thin. Earth's is also quite thick.

These four planets are called the terrestrial planets. That means they are like Earth.

The solar system

In the centre of our solar system is the Sun. The Sun is a star. It sends out the heat and light we call sunshine.

Mars

Jupiter

Freezing comets with long tails fly around the Sun, too.

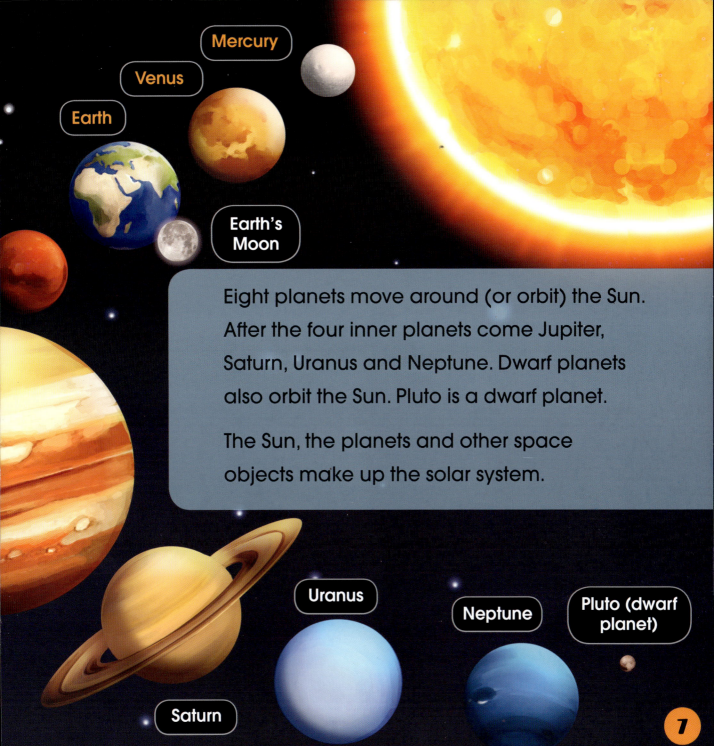

Mercury

Venus

Earth

Earth's Moon

Eight planets move around (or orbit) the Sun. After the four inner planets come Jupiter, Saturn, Uranus and Neptune. Dwarf planets also orbit the Sun. Pluto is a dwarf planet.

The Sun, the planets and other space objects make up the solar system.

Uranus

Neptune

Pluto (dwarf planet)

Saturn

Rocky worlds

Mercury, Venus, Earth and Mars are all made of rock. When these planets first formed they were very hot. Over millions of years, they cooled down. The surface of each planet formed a rocky crust.

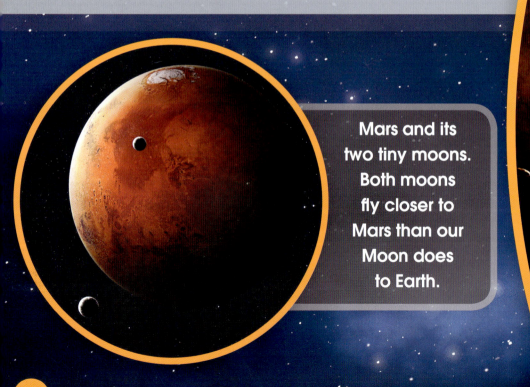

Mars and its two tiny moons. Both moons fly closer to Mars than our Moon does to Earth.

A moon is a piece of rock or ice that orbits a planet. Earth has one big moon. Mars has two tiny moons. Mercury and Venus have no moons.

Mercury

Mercury is the smallest planet orbiting the Sun. It travels faster than any other planet. Earth goes around the Sun in 365 days (one year). Mercury takes just 88 days!

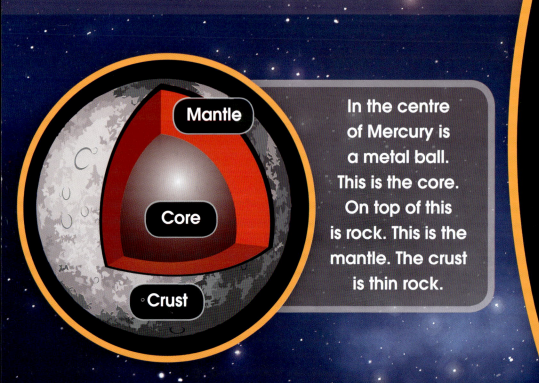

Mantle

Core

Crust

In the centre of Mercury is a metal ball. This is the core. On top of this is rock. This is the mantle. The crust is thin rock.

This photo shows
Mercury moving
in front of the Sun.

On the surface of Mercury is a thin crust of rock.
It has lots of shallow holes called craters. These
were made by space rocks crashing into it.

The side of Mercury that faces the Sun is very hot.
The other side is freezing cold.

Finding out about Mercury

Mercury is very hot because it is so close to the Sun. It can be 430°C on the surface! Only two spacecraft have visited. One, called *Mariner 10*, took photos of Mercury as it flew past.

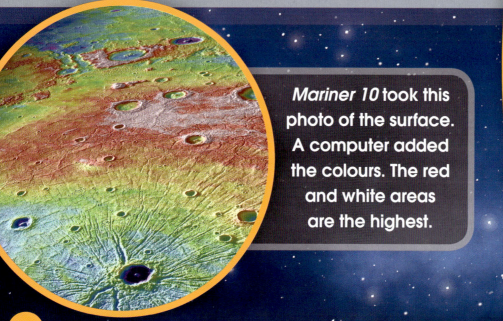

Mariner 10 took this photo of the surface. A computer added the colours. The red and white areas are the highest.

A space probe reached Mercury in 2011. It was called *Messenger*. It took photos and sent them back to Earth. In April 2015, *Messenger* crashed into Mercury's surface. Its mission was over.

WOW!
Messenger hit Mercury at more than 14,000 kph!

Messenger

Venus

Venus is the planet closest to Earth. It is about the same size as Earth. But it is very different. Venus is very hot. It is the hottest planet in the solar system. It is covered in thick, yellow clouds. They are full of acid.

Venus is the brightest object in Earth's night sky, apart from our Moon.

The Sun's light reflects off Venus's thick clouds. This makes Venus look very bright.

WOW!
Most planets, including Earth, spin to the right. Venus spins the other way. It turns towards the left.

Finding out about Venus

No one knew what Venus was like under the thick clouds. Robots that tried to land were destroyed in minutes. Then two space probes showed that Venus had lots of volcanoes.

The *Magellan* space probe made maps of the surface.

Most of the surface of Venus is covered in lava. This is a rock that comes out of volcanoes when they erupt.

Mars

Mars is the planet most like Earth.
It has clouds and winds. A long time
ago there might have been life on Mars.
But scientists have not found anything
living there today.

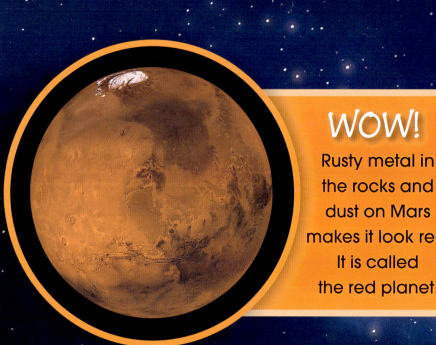

WOW!

Rusty metal in
the rocks and
dust on Mars
makes it look red.
It is called
the red planet.

Mars's bigger moon goes around it three times a day. The smaller one takes 30 hours to go around once.

There is a huge volcano on Mars. It is three times higher than the highest mountain on Earth, Mount Everest. Mars has two small moons. They are shaped like big potatoes.

Finding out about Mars

Lots of spacecraft have gone to Mars. They are looking for signs that something once lived there. Space rovers move over the surface and look at the rocks and soil. They take photos to send back to Earth.

A rover called *Curiosity* landed on Mars in 2012. Scientists operate the rover from Earth.

Curiosity is about the size of a car. It is driving over Mars to find out what the planet is like. In 2015 the rover found some big sand dunes. It sent photos of them back to Earth.

The planets and the Sun

What you need

Yellow, black and white paper
Coloured pencils

Pair of scissors
Paper fastener
Glue stick

What to do

1. Cut out a large black circle. Then cut out a small yellow circle (the Sun).

Mercury Venus Earth Mars Jupiter
Saturn Neptune Uranus

3. Copy and colour the planets. Cut them out.

2. Put the yellow circle on top of the black one. Push the paper fastener through the centre.

4. Stick the planets on the black paper, in order: Mercury, Venus, Earth, Mars, Jupiter, Saturn, Uranus and Neptune.

5. Hold the Sun still and watch the planets orbit the Sun.

Useful words

acid
A sour-tasting substance. Strong acids burn and are poisonous.

asteroid
A big rock that orbits the Sun. An asteroid can be just a few metres across, or hundreds of kilometres wide.

atmosphere
The layer of gases around a planet, moon or star.

comet
A ball of rock, dust and ice that orbits the Sun.

moon
An object in space that orbits a planet. Earth has one big moon. Mars has two small moons.

orbit
To move around another object.

planet
A large object in space that orbits the Sun or another star.

Sun
The star at the centre of the solar system.

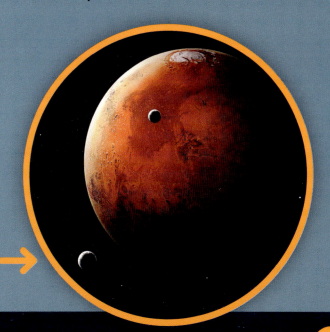

Find out more

Websites

www.esa.int/esaKIDSen/
Planetsandmoons.html

www.kidscosmos.org/mars/kids/
kids_basalt.php

www.planetsforkids.org/planet-
mercury.html

Books

First Fabulous Facts Space,
Anita Ganeri (Ladybird, 2014)

Solar System (DK Findout!),
(DK, 2016)

Index